Echo in Four Beats

poems by

Rita Banerjee

Finishing Line Press
Georgetown, Kentucky

Echo in Four Beats

Publication Acknowledgements:

Several of the poems featured in this manuscript have appeared in the chapbook *Cracklers at Night*, which received First Honorable Mention for Best Poetry Book in the 2012 Los Angeles Book Festival. *Cracklers at Night* (Finishing Line Press, 2010) was also featured on KBOO Radio's *APA Compass* (2011). Recordings of several poems appear in *Amethyst Arsenic, Quail Bell Magazine,* and *Hearsay Records,* and a podcast dedicated to Rita Banerjee's jazz poems appears on *Painted Bride Quarterly's* "Episode 27: Suicides and Skeleton Jazz" (Spring 2017). Some individual poems from the manuscript have been published in the following literary journals:

Academy of American Poets: Poem-a-Day: "Sleep" (November 30, 2017, Print and Recording)
Hyphen Magazine: "Ilha Formosa" (Spring 2017)
Painted Bride Quarterly: "Georgia Brown," "The Suicide Rag" (Podcast: Episode 27; Spring 2017; Issue 97, Print Annual 9: Summer 2018)
Mass Poetry Poem of the Moment: "Chicago Ode" (October 2016)
Queen Mob's Tea House: "Birds on Blue" (March 2016)
The Monarch Review: "Please Listen and Do Not Return," "Storyteller" (Fall 2015)
Riot Grrrl Magazine: "Pygmalion & the Slippers," "Currency" (August 2015)
Quail Bell Magazine: "Romani Folk Poem," "Kaddish," "A Hymn to Beauty," "Who Lamb" (Winter 2014 – Spring 2015, Print and Recordings)
Amethyst Arsenic: "America Ode" (Summer 2013, Print and Recording)
Dr. Hurley's Snake-Oil Cure: "Expectation" (Spring 2012)
Tupelo Press Million-Line Poem: "Small Berries" (Fall 2011)
Catamaran: "The Figure," "At Bougival" (Spring 2007)
The Dudley Review: "Didgeridoo, a Bird" (Spring 2007)
The Crab Creek Review: "The moon had jackknifed," (February 2007) 2006 Crab Pot Poetry Contest winner
Chrysanthemum: "For all that glitters..." (Spring 2006)
Objet d'Art: "Paper Men," "The half-penny sutra" (Spring 2004)
Hearsay Records: "Paper Men" (Recording, Spring 2004)

Publisher: Leah Maines
Editor: Christen Kincaid
Cover Art: Roxane van Beek
Author Photo: Nadja Teinze
Cover Design: Elizabeth Maines McCleavy

Printed in the USA on acid-free paper.
Order online: www.finishinglinepress.com
also available on amazon.com

Author inquiries and mail orders:
Finishing Line Press
P. O. Box 1626
Georgetown, Kentucky 40324
U. S. A.

Table of Contents

IV.

Acknowledgements
Biography

Für Stefan, meinen Lieblingsfaun—

I.

The moon had jackknifed,

broken mid-pace—
kept him still
pausing over an edgeless pool,
the orbs splitting yellow
spoke of oblivion,
his eyes glimmered,
the moon understood,
flew to him with haste,
first touching the cool palette
of his foot, then the sturdy
crest below his neck, finally
igniting in his wondrous eyes.
In the last spark,
his body gave way—
until nothing remained
but a lovely blank
and the windshield
warped by the embrace.

The Figure

*"We find beauty not in the thing itself
but in the patterns of shadows."*
— *Jun-ichirō Tanizaki*

I only understood by casting you
first in flesh, then in clay,
and finally in frail, sea-water words.
You tendered there—
adrift on the tide
and I had to cast you out again
like a net, hoping to catch
in your sprawling,
some aquatic thing,
some solace that would heal the lines
between blue and continent.
That's what I found in you
the day you stood again beside me
and the sun poured out from the sky.

At Bougival

(after Pierre-Auguste Renoir)

The old harbor drained of tea has no dream
and cobblestone streets when strummed
speak silver. In a narrow gully hums
a pitted house; on weekends it receives
the weary-eyed. Welcomes, there, seem
hollow when held high and numbed
by coffered chandeliers. But the kind host thumbs
them out and then abandons guests to dream

to discover in the study: paintings, plaques,
and their confessions. Centered in faux glass,
a couple careens and is caught mid-glance.
The man, half-hatted, stops and pulls her back,
but the red-bonnet girl glides through the glass,
her motion naïve, her misstep a dance.

Creation Hymn I[1]
(after Ovid)

Throughout all
Aonian cities:
faultless answers—

Dusky Naiad,
the first to test
the truth,

the loveliest of
nymphs, gave birth
to a child

whom, even then,
one could
fall in love with

Narcissus
both boy and youth
the strangeness

of his passion,
delicate form
Echo saw him

she, who cannot be
silent, might learn how
to speak first herself

---

[1] Erasure poem based on A.S. Kline's translation of Ovid's *The Metamorphoses.*

Pygmalion & the Slippers

I.

Dusty books, gramophones,
wooden panes,
for every umlaut,
there was rain, and shadows
crossing ceilings.

For every moving shade,
there was a jewel,
a bunt cake,
tea with honey,
rubies, too,
found them dead in a village
near the Ganges,
in some bastard king's chest.

Just six beads for all
of Manhattan, just six
vowels in the bidder's language
but how many aspirations for plain?

Diphthong, dental, dental—
the orthography of the primitives
has shown that six vowels in combination
with six men will lead to a triptych.

French: *ménage à trois*
Father, son, and—
popular imagination says
that we the people of kingdom come
phylum chordata class none
order lost genius some
are not people but
the feminine

noun in German has
few declensions
*Rotkäppchen, siehst du
die schönen großen Blumen?*

How to say "ahh"
without falling?
Rotkäppchen—
Red, her face in rain,
what falls against
the window pane.
In Spain, there are
tildes, conquistadores,
and Don Quixote still

chasing windmills
and his girl-princess.
Princess, stick a ruler on
your tongue, and bite,
remove when numbed,
let English speak,
let the English

II.

Why does light outside
a dark window
always want
to dance patterns
as if to say
as if to say
her body is written

by your clever
her mind forgotten
by proper
As per the fall?

Noun declensions,
diminutives, original
sin? She's no siren,
her sin not original
but stick a ruler on her

tongue, let the ships
crash, swallow-song,
English straight
shoe lace, strung her words
tight like riding boots.

Odysseus, why are you?
Riding books,
funny her words

but she came back,
so why fear? Goddess
immaculate, Virgin
Mary, too, her single form
in clay, her smile not
unbecoming, so why
do you bid her to speak,
to fetch a pair of shoes?

Currency

In Black Rock City,
desert law proclaims:
liberation's a bear dance,
no cash, no transactions.
Fire embracing fire obliterates
we chant, leaves no trace—
a man without desert
has no home. Around us
they gather, counting ducks,
hens, any feather will do.
They build a phoenix to live
on ashes, but when we rise,
we rise all fur and teeth.
In Nevada, the stars throw
down their silver bounty
to the bear dancing on one leg,
and when the sky comes down
to devour us, it rains in quarters.

America Ode

not sound not
voice in that
hollow

how to keep
a weapon of
choice, ricochet

late nights dried
neon, our drinks
were made

from smooth
paste, the sun too
I saw

beautiful
outside the
mirror, hard to

know
the world,
leaves in a

mirror, the ice
in my vodka
reflected

the screen
dead blue,
on late night

news, they were
showing men
raw and packed

in ice, red
not my fault
the news had said

like fish
we thought
they could swim

they would
not
like us

newsman smiled,
newwoman too,
late night vodka

on white sheet
ice relieves
what might,

suicide shot,
the billiard ball
nothing more

in this merry
go merry
go round

laughter,
the red drum
stirred, hung

all those yellow
hearts packed
'em tight and kept

them in form
aldehyde,
numb liquid,

we drank up
and kept what
thoughts we made

kept ourselves
walking through
the valley

through
this shadow
land of ours

and saw no evil.

Please Listen and Do Not Return
(after Nick Carraway and Tom Joad)

East

She, portrait
in miniature, she
I said I had

found in my youth
a her, a when
men built dreams

with hands
still, I saved
a lock of hers, kept

her like the harbor
lights, ship sounds
at night, I knew

light, green-back
and otherwise
could bring me

closer—
to that mind
daffodil colored—

I wondered again the
meaning of East,
the mean,

what emotions went
with living,
with home

things travel
through valleys
of ash, I walk

in gray
and dead houses,
her eyes porcelain

undirected
like mint
limited

always close
always closed
to me

     West

She's full stamped
on ground
my fingers

drew the line out
before the turtle
came to

dust to dust
my world
was thin

I had no roam
no hope to
call a

road, a line
that would
take

she aired
full of whistle
like brakes, she came

to me like
my sister
what could I—

knot her hair,
braid its rust
and mettle

she held the imprints
of children
in her, held

nothing more
like Saturn,
her orchards

too far to know
what fruit
of home could and

in what river
slots we'd find
the used

jalopies, family
was not
a word I had

seen on the chalky
road-signs, in the
magazines

used jalopy
yoked
separate

couldn't buy
what I didn't
earn, earth

to ghosts to
graves, her eyes
gave milk.

Chicago Ode

You came quiet on
cat feet with
disregard
for minor names

Like architecture,
you remained
aortal and stung—

Colors dropped
off grids and arcs,
bending like yellow,
red and unglued blue

You moved like
a river under
Boul Mich, elevated
trains

undulated space,
kept sails and lovers
lit on harbor

like bodies lit
on grass, you stood
unlike bronze

unlike concrete, too
contained in no
form, no limb
that would move

like fever
your eyes grew
catlike, calling to
strange bodies,

locking lakes in land,
you asked time to
sneeze, hiccup, to not
speak at all—

asked to linger no
longer or to
stay longer like

cracklers at night,
the firework's parched
breath & Ferris wheel
lights that held

like ships & whistles
a cradle
without thread.

For all that glitters…

Love is the throw of stone on water—the skip,
flight, and longed-for collapse, gravel shot to slip.

Love is the bird turned on its eye, plume soaking
in red, wind cooling smoke from a barrel tip.

Love is a high-beam walk, platform shrinking
to wire space, foot, flinching up, poised to trip.

Love is a coin tossed in a well—gold sinking
through black, a stuttering flash lost in the dip.

Love is being caught on mountains, looking
for light, hearths burning as distant diamond chips.

Love is to break ordinary stones, searching
for fire, only to find a dew on their lips.

Thanatos

Lie down, you say, next to me
and we will talk as men and women do

There will be gold, and amber,
and green as deep as the Birnam woods

We will let the sun strike
through the panes of our church

We will supplicate, sublime, and let
our bodies dance through reverence.

The Suicide Rag

Billy played ragtime
on the church
organ but we

lunch-hour kids,
kept time by another
name. Behind St. Augustine's

we learned to hit
the pavement, sound
like an anvil

crack
hammers hitting
steel, Billy playing

skeletons
on the fifth,
we arpeggioed

haloed, froze
on the black
top. Learning

to cakewalk
This was our
battle—

tar-mat babies
doing handsprung
suicides

for the girls
standing 'round
with knife-like eyes

That's all
we needed—
a rolling

beat, a firing squad
and schoolyard
skirts

scouring the lot
as we fell
face forward

hands locked
& stiff, the only
thing

that could've
come between
us was a kiss.

Georgia Brown

Harlem had yet to be born,
the globe had not been spun,
but we knew how to whistle,
how to call clappers and skirts on cue:
That summer, we first met Georgia,
she was an echo in four beats,
we learned to hum her story.
Mike played her with a licked reed
but she was all brass, sharp
like an abandoned railroad cutting through
wild wood, and when she took stage,
she made those trombone boys whisper,
"Sweet Georgia, Sweet."

Birds on Blue

*"Is it not sweet to think that, if only you have patience,
all that has ever been will come back to you?"*
—Isak Dinesen

If liberty were jazz, she'd be waiting
like a crow, keeping crown
on ebony wings, mapping out
America over ocean.

Crow found jazz on an island atoll,
she was praying for China Blue
when it blasted—

Crow's heart needs a container,
innocence a hearth,
and Little Boy a beat.

Little Boy runs around hen-pen
waiting to crow like
a rooster with his head cut

Crow-bird sallies, keeps the mood

Rooster's a hand-grenade,
Crow's trumpet cool,
blue words contain her,

Not Rooster, he's searching
for a way to speech—

だまれ！！
He's up then collapses
on little crow feet.

On fine dark wings,
Crow-bird rehearses,
lets her voice run vertical

over men, over fire, over sea,
when her song finally reaches America,
it thumps a sky glazed porcelain

Creation Hymn II[2]

(after Ovid)

Echo had a body then
not merely a voice,
when Saturnia realized this

she said, "I shall give you
less power
over that tongue—"

Echo burned with fire,
sulphur,
her nature denies it,

she is ready for what
it will allow her to do:
to wait for sounds

---

[2] Erasure poem based on A.S. Kline's translation of Ovid's *The Metamorphoses.*

II.

Atlantis

The sun shone brilliant
over the diamond curves of the water.

The air tasted heavy of salt. It was a changeling season—
the albatross had not yet wandered towards the bay

but the seagulls were dancing already
on the winter weed. They had broken

the hard-shelled animals by their seams,
cracked spines with a flash of light.

The parking lot was filled with seaside smells
and the scent of unknown creatures. The gulls murmured

their delight. The sand shimmied and tapered,
fringing into the water at the most inopportune moments—

My camera held the scene, set like some actor's living room
stage. Everything was quiet, white, ordinary, bright—

My fingers traced out the shipwrecked den, there was gold
in the bottom rungs of the sunken ship, in the glint

of a rusted harpoon which glowed underneath the shifting tide,
as if it were some sort of diurnal lamp.

We were like that— lanterns in the midday sun,
laughter against a white-noise wind, tongues

circling salt-water stories, cliffs cocooned by the afternoon, cameras
catching harbor fish, reptiles, serpents, impossible possibilities—

We were like that, like two roads diverging on a cool spring day
where the winter had lefts its sympathy,

And we took the one that curved and mistook
and stumbled onto ocean, ocean, ocean.

Ilha Formosa

Under the synthetic pop,
there's a drum like the slow pace
of an old tin fan turning round
and round in its socket, propelling
a cool metal breeze to wander

around and casually finger the back
of the neck—There is something balmy
and unsettled here, as if the island knows
more than sulfur and air and water shift
between earth and its beautiful blue fringe—

From aerial height, the eye wanders over
and almost misses this small cove
of verdant green rising up from the sea.
It is easy to get lost in the South Pacific,
to fall into the rhythm of the blood-beat
that echoes under the murmur of currents—

This is the island's mesmer spell:
to look into the mirror of a mountain
and see your own face grown thick
in the moss, and the eyes pointing back at you:
wild, marbled, and reptilian—

Sleep

What does it mean to be so still?
to glide along the ocean floor

like some black-tongued electric eel,
to burn through marbled gold and green

of oceanic things like some
compact mass deforming space, time,

a void within voids, and then?
It is easier to imagine amphibian,

to know that blood, too, can change
its temperament as quickly as

salamanders change skin, as quickly as
eyes of newt and tongues of dog become

incantations, enchantments of art
and life just as an animal submerged

under water becomes unknown,
just as respirations become primitive

and breaths and motions cease
as a lone fish in a dark pond

arrives as an object of thought
and becomes stone.

Sustenance Hymn I[3]
(after Ovid)

He is astonished,
glances everywhere
no one appearing

Her voice, her bones,
shapes of stone heard
by everyone: sound lives in her

---

[3] Erasure poem based on A.S. Kline's translation of Ovid's *The Metamorphoses*.

Après-demain

I had stored them in the cupboards,
in the sleeves of record albums,
pinned under cushions, carved
inside artichoke hearts—

Sometimes I hid them under banisters,
in sheets of fresh linen, or rolled up
in the dust, I kept them like seeds
from my green clementine tree,

muted like rain stamping rivers 'cross
the kitchen windows, I hid them under
potted plants, safely within deposit boxes,
buried in earth like time capsules—

And once, I hid them in the best place of all:
within plain sight, between the curve and dip
of hastily scribbled letters, within the erratic, roaming
lines of my second-hand typewriter—

kept them behind the surface of
breaths and people, between lives
and their punctuations,

but they could only stay for so long in a cabinet,
in a witty joke or cup of tea—

One day, I noticed, like sugar, they came
pouring out, one crystalline spoonful
at a time, and when I opened my doors and looked

within those cracked walls and cushioned things,
I realized that all my jars of glass and thought,
all those hiding places I thought safe

were empty, and all the things I had kept hidden
were gone, and there were no tomorrows left anymore.

Object

(after Jangarh Singh Shyam)

Last night
I found myself
wandering

down the underground
alleyways that led
to the mouth of hell—

The door was
inscribed in
simple French:

*Arrête! C'est ici
l'empire de la mort.*

I see you, thing,
lying there covered
in black fichu

and simple white
lace, and I think
death has a way

of following us,
of waiting at the table,
sometimes on it.

Death is a pile
of human bones
artfully arranged

into perfect
concentric
grids, as if

human lives
are perfect three-
dimensional squares

of time. I could stare
at an old rotting
skull in the glow

of torch-light and wonder
at the stitching
across its cranium.

This is where
two plates meet:
almost tectonic

as if our very bones
are continents
colliding.

I could stare
at you, thing,
covered and cold

on the table, and I would
get no sense of motion,
not even in death.

Last night I saw
the branching horns
and seaward lines

of a creature, half gazelle,
half magic stretched
across a canvas.

The lines of fur,
like Japanese rice
paper, were printed

and stained to look
like fireworks
at a summer festival.

I wanted to wear
my kimono
at the celebration

of your gallery
opening. I would
have been there

in front of the prints
and their animal shapes
and shadows

waiting for you
to appear, hoping
to uncover

something, but you
would not arrive. The plaque
about you would say

you had disappeared,
gone undercover,
lost ten years ago.

Storyteller

(after Gloria Rich)

words depend
on the breath
between

my voice and yours,
on the mist
that streams

between two mouths
staring at each other
in a lone alleyway

in the dark cool eve
of winter in the bright city
with a kaleidoscope

belly. The breaths
between lips are mixing,
the mouths are black

holes, craving light
and each other.
They are hungry—

they want to kiss
the whiteness
between words,

devour silence and its fruits.

The Conversation

(after Jivya Soma Mashe)

At one pole, lady with a gourd of water
tugs on the woven cloth
that makes the world.

On the other, lady with a fireball
makes a string, and pulls up
another pole.

They catch in their netting crabs, rice, salamanders—
sometimes snakes and verdant creepers.

Outside on their tympanic net, humans wander
trying to ensnare fish and air,
trying to charm each other through the lattices

The women are speaking
to one another, building
empires of ants and grains.

The sky is a muddied brown, but
their lives are defined by white
lines, white lies, and white

                    noise.

白魔法[4] (White Magic)

It is so cold in Kyōto,
it is easy to break off fingers
like branches, one crystalline
blade at a time:

So cold, the breath stops.
Frost mars the window,
the glass is etched
with dust and demons.

So cold that it is easy to
wander through zebra crossings,
through temples and rock-
garden parks, forgetting time:

Forgetting one's mother
tongue, forgetting everything
but the bite of ice on lips,
of winter licking serpents on lashes:

It is so cold in Kyōto,
it is easy to forget
How to breathe

when the first snow of winter,
the first snow ever witnessed *falls*

in sleeting, spindling streams:

Spiking palms, covering copper
roofs, shifting over temple gates
and quiet oaks, falling softly
through bamboo

       groves, on red
maples, glittering over dark,
wet-vapor camphor trees—

---

[4] 白魔法 ("Shiromahō") means "white magic" in Japanese.　　39

水の音

深い
葉の多い井戸
利口で若い蛙
鉄条網の天
全然飛び出さない

A Water's Sound[5]

Deep,
    a leaf-grown well,
  wise young toad
a wire-meshed sky,
      never will jump.

---

[5] 水の音 ("Mizu no Oto," "A Water's Sound") was originally written in Japanese by Rita Banerjee and is translated into English by Rita Banerjee.

Sustenance Hymn II [6]

    (after Ovid)

He loves a bodiless dream—
hangs motionless,
he is astonished by

himself, carved from Parian marble,
he contemplates
two stars, fit

for Bacchus, fit for Apollo
rose-flush,
he inflames and burns

unknowingly he desires
himself, error
seduces and deceives

---

[6] Erasure poem based on A.S. Kline's translation of Ovid's *The Metamorphoses.*

Diver

What did the first pearl diver see
as he stared deep into that ocean among oceans?

Did he search for some solid form, some *shard* of stardust
or stone to call a diamond or some other word

for *home*? Did he seek its brilliance or did he seek
that thing which would not shine, which did not *reflect* his image

among the earth's infinite fractals? Did he search for some cool, hard figure
that was *soft* to the touch but heavy to carry

like the years that slipped through and shimmered in his mind,
like the glow of some distant green dockside lantern?

Did this thing he sought *drink in* light by accident, through the mouth,
deep in the underbelly of the ocean?

Was it the only thing that said: "Diver, you have seen your face
mirrored in a hundred forms, now see *mine*"

Onsen

There is nothing like
swimming naked

in the dead of winter
when the pavement is covered

over, littered over with frost—

The fields are fleece
white, and the sky is falling

to pieces overhead—

There is nothing like
swimming naked

in quiet snowstorms,
outdoors

in an *ofuro* meant for walking

Amour-propre

Only the eyes: yours
so like mine, can
speak, sting—

III.

Bacchanalia

I spent thirty years of my life climbing
up stairs, reaching landings and tripping
down them, like ones and zeroes, there
was an infinite rhythm to my steps,

they formed whole words and fell in line
like dictation, it was easy to move
backwards or forwards in binary
like a dancer in some modern day *ballet*

mécanique, like a spell that kept
uttering its own incantation,
like Faust, so afraid to stop for a while—

What does it take to make a moment?
to take a breath and stop for a minute
without intention? I've spent too many
hours and too many miles searching

for those lines that make up the world's warp
and woof, that can spin yarns for centuries
to come or that sing honestly of centuries long ago—

Sometimes it's not easy to move forward,
and sometimes it's too easy to go back,
so why not try something syncopated?

Why not spill sideways, slip
and dishevel? Why not spend a moment
on a wayward thought or give into babble?

Why not live in gyroscopic time?
and spend the next thirty years
with two left feet, like Dionysus, and in trouble?

Destruction Hymn I [7]

> *(after Ovid)*

"We are apart *only*
by a little water!"
Strange prayer for a lover,

lips to me, you would think
he could be touched,
when I smile, you

smile back. All my riches
make me poor: he desires
to be held.

---

[7] Erasure poem based on A.S. Kline's translation of Ovid's *The Metamorphoses*.

Romani Folk Poem[8]

Salve Roma, save, Soul Roma—
some call me Roma
or a killer
or a killer,
defiant killer,
my love's dying
my love's defying,
my love's dying
idyllically…

Soul Roma… dying
Soul Roma, papa, papa, is dying
idyllically, see—
idyllically, see—
Soul Roma's dying

---

[8] A "mis-translation" of "Ederlezi," a Romani folk poem.

A Hymn to Beauty [9]

(after Charles Baudelaire)

A sleeping room:
the debasement is a filter,
the sleep's an error,
sort through the comfort.
The courageous woman,
the Seine's overturned with disaster—

Disaster? That's nothing!
the hour's not charming,
the monster allows sleep &
the dead plant: the dance of love,
beautifully flaming enormous
monster & a frying ingénue

The feet, finally, I know
orange compote: the love I knew—
Fake azure, red phantom,
the liver on the bed
in an instant, I think, is disaster

---

[9] A "mis-translation" of Charles Baudelaire's "Hymne à la beauté."

Who lamb[10]

Who lamb.
Who's into who lamb?
Igor likes Congo Music,
Caress my photo, who lamb.
He said Marion bring me a who lamb,
Sheared.

Azaleas on the bank,
Hollow as eggs
On the bank

Best who lamb with chocolate
Seismic who lamb
Igor likes to pay
For it with
Who lamb
Who lamb
Who lamb

---

[10] A "mis-translation" of Diana Norma Szokolyai's poem "hullám/wave."

Didgeridoo, a Bird

(for James Lechner & Susan Parr)

Foam tide occi-dental
         dontal dollop—
  oop! went the ocean
festoons, pistons, and drunk.

Didgeridoo the ancient
      the mermaid's burp,
she bird, sine bird
   trying to fold flat, then run,
scraping circumlocutions,
        steady waves.

Billow, billow,
    the hummingbird's hurt!
landed at my feet, She did,
   all covered in mink, a-faux.

Frozen-spot foe,
  the fiendish be right
humbird's nervous, nervous
    found somethin in her image
sustained waves, she says,
      waverin imagination.

Can't fold flat,
  little bird, siren's wop;
got her tresses in a mess,
     (cantankerous)
looking for a thought, she is
   sustained elocution,
  been trying to execute,
    but she hung
       in execution.

Kaddish[11]

It's gold, it's Kaddish,
a chimera. My mother decides:
it's over.

Mercurial,
the bird is burnt.
overturn Israel. be my god.

Carry the fever:
amen.

A man shivers bare, or the maze almanacs,
lightning strikes—

Be it Roman, be it Tatar, be it Allah,
or blood

On roads, bare-hoofed:
broken

---

[11] A "mis-translation" of a Hebrew prayer.

Destruction Hymn II[12]
(after Ovid)

He saw it vanishing,
"Stay, cruel one!"
I am allowed to gaze

at what I cannot touch,
white mingled with red,
that form so pleasing

that which Echo loved,
"Alas!" she repeated.
In vain, he laid

his weary head, but
there was no body, instead:
white petals, a flower, a yellow heart.

---

[12] Erasure poem based on A.S. Kline's translation of Ovid's *The Metamorphoses.*

Eros

In this version
of myth, Echo and
Narcissus are never meant

to talk, to listen
and recognize
not just their own

desire
but the human
gesture, the need

reflected in
sex and response,
in repose,

in each other
In this story, only
the masculine can be

divine, and
the feminine
eternally divided—

In this myth, Narcissus
is not meant to look
backwards

over one fine shoulder,
chiseled, torquing his torso
so that every part

of his skin glows
to see you. Echo is not
meant to be seen

in her careless dress
and maddening hair,
the gauze of her gown:

opaque, golden, woven
is just another kind of fire
against the skin.

Narcissus, more animal now
than man or flower, is not
supposed to stir

from his laurel throne, not
supposed to abandon the mirror
of the lake, and kneel

on all fours, changing
his skin
in the dappled light

leopard, feline, famished—
and ready to play
predator,

the girl with the wild hair
and golden robes is not
meant to be hunted,

she who is no white fawn,
she who is not
an object

of enchantment,
of caress,
she who gazes

the way women do,
no topaz locket
garlanding her throat—

That's not how we play
this game, Echo thinks
but does not speak

"Say what you will
to me," Narcissus dares,
hiding neither fur

nor teeth. "You will,"
her words come
too late, "what you will,"

she who is not
meant to be just
a woman—

A flower can bloom
but a man
has other methods,

the line of his lips
is incantatory,
they motion and beg

until she speaks.

IV.

Expectation

(after Gustav Klimt)

She is a woman
of triangle and circle,
made of curled fog
and rolling squares—

I want to hold her there
on my tongue, and know
what the shape and shine
of gold tastes like.

Small Berries:

I bought a box
of strawberries today.

They were ripe & they
were tart.

I would like to share them
with you.

But not
the satisfaction—

Paper Men

xeroxing epiphanies at 5¢ a page, the messiah standing next to me has been speaking the word of hope and rage for 37 years. with 4000 books living in his mind, he's international, a sage who hands me a song of California. and anaheim—anaheim—been on my mind for seven straight minutes. why? 7 for luck and anaheim for memories not mine. brushing the tattoo of a carnivale, he says there isn't a circus in the world he hasn't been to. and he'd like to be called Nesmith if you don't mind. and when he says Nesmith, i think of mike and white out. white out morning after crash— seven days of meditating Tantric verse and I crashed, crashed for six long hours at the highest level of understanding and do you understand me, child, when I say, I cannot describe it to you? the Supreme spoke to me and I had something to say. and this I've said for years. and when his eyes ask, believe me, i do 'cause there isn't a story i haven't believed in. and when i nod yes, he says, I have found in your eyes a kindred spirit. and i think of the paper man i once met on an island. in my back-pocket wallet, the name Yoshida's inked, hand-pressed on rice-white paper. Yoshida sighed once, look at the color of our women—hair the color of the sun— there is no space for dark anymore. just the shade of this paper store and the wait, the wait for a word-maker to pass by. and so he tells me of Korea, the blasphemy of emperors disgraced, and the beauty of his wife when she wakes him. we talk and talk and talk of the greatness of rome, sartre, and curry. and somehow beneath the talk, i can hear his heart. and tonight after kissing another man of verse, i walk down white halls with a book of words on my head, and think. today, i met a poet.

Lumière

On the night
          of the falling moon,
I saw an atomic round:

it was deep
          and exploded
without a rhyming sound:

in the dark,
          it echoed
like a beacon & a curse:

in the moonless
          night, it metered *orange*

On Dharma[13]

> *(after Gina La Piana)*

Busker mama,
yesterday came.

She came
like an aspirin photo
and hung the day
like a cat.

The limoncello took part
in the show,
it was, as we say, a comma.

Come time again
and momma no say.
I'm gonna say: tomato
I'm gonna say: so much

I say to papa: the wishes
come to stay.

---

[13] A "mis-translation" of a poem in "Gina Language."

एक रात में [14]

मैंने एक रात बारिश के हज़ार नाच सुने
चूड़ी की तरह आकाश टुकड़े टुकड़े हो गया
गली के आइने में पृथ्वी उलटी लगी
पानी के हिलने से सब दुनिया बदलने लगी
और मेरी तस्वीर भी दूसरी हो गई
चारों तरफ़ आकाश के नाच में
असली दुनिया नक़ली लगने लगी
और पानी के एक एक टुकड़े में
चाँद हँस रहा था।

One Night

One night I heard the thousand
dances of rain—

like a bangle, the sky broke
                into pieces

in the mirror of the alley,
the earth looked up-

side-down, the world kept
transforming

in the moving
water, my face, too, became another—

from all four directions, in the sky's
dance, the world appeared

unreal, and in each broken piece of water,
the moon remained, laughing—

---

[14] एक रात में ("Ek Rāt Mem," "One Night") was originally written in Hindi by
Rita Banerjee and has been translated into English by Rita Banerjee.

The half-penny sutra

If the mind is a half-gleaned eidolon,
    the world will be found in its absence.
If there is smoke rising from a mountain's top,
    the sun will be snuffed out behind it.
If there are two birds sitting on a tree,
    one will gaze at the other and devour it.
If a chariot is rumbling through the streets,
    even admirers will take care to avoid it.
If a rope can be mistaken for a snake,
    the more profit its charmer will make.
If five blind men feel an elephant's hide,
    they'll touch the truth but speak the lie.

Beyond Saṃsāra

In the Glyptothek,
the sunlight hits
the marble

in all angles.
The light is blue
but far from cold

On this mid-winter morning,
we are three fates:
women, writers, artists—

Our feet, lined
with faux leather
and fur, mark

paw-like prints
on the white grass,
on black-ice stairs

In the Glyptothek,
we unravel,
throwing off our veils

and scarves and gloves
and glue, one layer
of enchantment

dispels another.
Finally, we're left
in just our combat boots,

books and pens,
naked
but not enough.

The great halls
are domed silver-
white stalactites

and the statues placed
at their centers,
provocative

upward-bound
stalagmites. Between marble
and marble

are digital screens,
and mixed-media collages
of what ancient Rome

and Greece
may in the future
look like

many images curl
in magenta
and rendezvous pink,

all lips and ire.
When we, oracles,
fates, women finally grace

upon the Barberini Faun,
we are not startled
by his spectacle,

made breathless
by his repose, or struck
by the light that

glides off each curve
and crest of his
naked form—

But we are entranced
by his complete
abandon, his zealous

amour-propre,
his pleasure in auto-
eroticism.

Amahl, who composes plays
about transgender Arabs
and who is fleeing Jordan,

casts her words at me:
"Look how much he loves
himself."

"He's so decadent, so free,"
Sabine chimes at my side,
her spectacles flashing.

Barberini in marble
is an absolute libertine
and just as alluring

for his self-abandon,
all passion and giddy
self-absorption—

"I'd like to be so decadent,
so free," I jest, just by half.
Amahl returns my gaze,

Sabine breaks it, one
of us smiles through the whisper
"then be free"

রেলগাড়ী (Railcars)

Howrah

Subterranean warship,
iceberg, catastrophe,
the train slid in, armored

in rust and sulfur,
titanic. Impossible

it would not hit
the wall. The wall
sprocketed, out-browned

by time, sought to
collide with this living

beast. But those living
stayed their own
games—chewed betel

leaf, printed newspapers
on cellophane, made coolies

carry blue elephants,
hand bags, attachés—

piled them high with thin
hands, keeping the weight
of worlds aloft like moons

eclipsed by immovable locks.

Manipal

My first train was a taste
a touch of tart on tongue,

the kind of sour that comes
with heavy air, forms

around giants, red-iron
oxcarts, palm trees—

whole villages passing
by perforated windows

no difference between
languages, signs, the names

of things, or how the dust
pools red in Ranchi,

redder in Vizag than
all the concrete steps

to my San Francisco
home— Nani, her

starry voice carried
make believe, home-

spun kings, invisible cloths,
and spiced lunch-hour

dishes of spinach
and sour rice with just

a trace of fairytale

Nainital

It took only one
roach and then an
echo to know

the entire train was
infested with small shellacked

creatures. Their glistening
wings smelled of gasoline,
hard-metal moonshine—

I could only hear the buzz,
the only image drunk enough
to utter a sound, disturb

the constant hum of falling
tracks, charging wheels.

The two bunk beds
kept mum, snapped
tight like clams,

cool as sand dollars
collected by the tide,

the walls muted
in sea-moss between
each flying rice paddy,

where each leaf suspended
on water's sky-line silver,
indicating rain as smoke

below mountains indicated life
existed in small thatched huts

beside cooking pyres,
gray ash and hypnotizing
pink embers. It was getting cold,

colder. The palm trees,
banana leaves had disappeared

But the clouds gathered dark—
somewhere on a field
in the middle of Bharat

stood a black girl
with black doe eyes,

her hair a catastrophe
caused by the wind. The clouds
stood court above her,

it took no gods here
to call thunder, to recite

the poem of the girl,
sing *que sera sera*

remember old faces, old
honeymoon trips, and their
chromatic colors, her first taste

of custard apple in the gardens
of old Ranchi, laughter, family

and their albums, the only
kinds of commotion
needed to sway cars, keep

propelling as the train
reaching the foothills of

the Himalayas, broke silence.

Acknowledgements

Several poets and writers have guided me on this journey through the myths of Echo and Narcissus, music, politics, and America. Thank you to Richard Kenney, Colleen McElroy, Heather McHugh, Linda Bierds, Robert Hass, Jorie Graham, Jeanne Marie Beaumont, and Helen Vendler for your generous support and feedback on early drafts of my work. Thanks to Maya Sonenberg, Darcy Frey, Srikanth Reddy, Patrick Rosal, Kate Flint, Douglas Piccinnini, Claire Henderson, *Objet d'Art*, Kazim Ali, Erik Kennedy, Kathleen Spivack, Gregory Crosby, Lisa Yarger, Mark Olival-Bartley, the Munich Writers, Samantha Milowsky, Jake Uitti, Koon Woon, Elizabeth Devlin, Jen Benka, Kevin Larimer, and Mary Gannon for being wonderful readers and advocates of my work. Thanks to Usha Jain for encouraging me to write in Hindi, and Indra Levy for encouraging me to write in Japanese. Thanks to Wings, the Star Life on the Oasis, and my fellow artists in Seattle for providing so much inspiration. Many thanks to my editors Leah Maines and Christen Kincaid for your insight and generosity, and to Roxane van Beek and Elizabeth Maines McCleavy for the gorgeous cover design. Thank you, Natalie Kimber, for being a rock-star agent and a truly luminous human being. Many thanks to Diana Norma Szokolyai, Dennis Shafer, and the Cambridge Writers' Workshop for creating a space for electric art. Thanks much to my lovely parents, Gargi and Tapan, and to Nani, Dadabhai, Moni, Dada, and all of my family and friends for your encouragement, love, and inspiration. Thank you, David, for being the provocateur I needed. And a special thank you and much love to Stefan for opening my eyes.

Rita Banerjee is the editor of *CREDO: An Anthology of Manifestos and Sourcebook for Creative Writing* (C&R Press, May 2018) and the author of the poetry collection *Echo in Four Beats* (Finishing Line Press, March 2018), which was a finalist for the Red Hen Press Benjamin Saltman Award, Three Mile Harbor Poetry Prize, and Aquarius Press / Willow Books Literature Award, the novella "A Night with Kali" in *Approaching Footsteps* (Spider Road Press, 2016), and the poetry chapbook *Cracklers at Night* (Finishing Line Press, 2010). She earned her doctorate in Comparative Literature from Harvard and her M.F.A. in Creative Writing from the University of Washington, and her work appears in the *Academy of American Poets, Poets & Writers, Nat. Brut., The Rumpus, The Scofield, Hyphen Magazine, Electric Literature, Painted Bride Quarterly, VIDA: Women in Literary Arts, Los Angeles Review of Books*, and elsewhere. She is the Executive Creative Director of the Cambridge Writers' Workshop and an Associate Scholar of Comparative Literature at Harvard University, and teaches on modernism, art-house film, and South Asian literary theory at the Ludwig Maximilian University of Munich in Germany. She is the judge for the 2017 Minerva Rising "Dare to Speak" Poetry Chapbook Contest, and she is currently working on a novel about a Tamil-Jewish American family in crisis during a post-authoritarian regime, a book on South Asian literary modernisms, a documentary film about race and intimacy in the United States and in France, and a collection of essays on race, sex, politics, and everything cool.

CPSIA information can be obtained
at www.ICGtesting.com
Printed in the USA
BVHW07s0934121018
529910BV00003B/1143/P